*Presented to:*

_____

*Presented by:*

_____

*Date:*

_____

# CELEBRATE EASTER!

## HONOR HB BOOKS

*Inspiration and Motivation for the Season of Life*

An Imprint of Cook Communications Ministries • Colorado Springs, CO

08 07 06 05 04        10 9 8 7 6 5 4 3 2 1

*Celebrate Easter: Stories, Quotes, and Poems to Inspire a Joyous Season!*
ISBN 1-56292-179-7
Copyright © 2004 by Bordon Books
6532 E. 71st Street, Suite 105
Tulsa, OK 74133

Published by Honor Books
An imprint of Cook Communication Ministries
4050 Lee Vance View
Colorado Springs, CO 80918

Developed by Bordon Books

Manuscript compiled by Snapdragon Editorial Group, Inc.

# Introduction

The Easter season is one of the most glorious in the Christian faith—the pivotal point of our faith and hope. Along with the angels of heaven and believers throughout the ages, Easter is a time to celebrate the risen Lord—Jesus Christ!

Ours is not a dead religion; there is no sacred burial place. Instead, we dance and shout in celebration of an *empty* tomb, *abandoned* grave clothes, and *a Savior who conquered death* on our behalf.

We hope the quotes, scriptures, poetry, and traditions included in this little book will inspire you, touch your heart, and make you feel like celebrating. It was designed to help you fully enter into the greatest celebration of all!

*Celebrate God's Victorious Goodness!*
*God is good and God is light,*
*In this faith I rest secure,*
*Evil can but serve the right,*
*Over all shall love endure.*

*Christ has risen! Hallelujah!*
*Blessèd morn of life and light!*
*Lo, the grave is rent asunder,*
*Death is conquered through His might.*

*Christ is risen! Hallelujah!*
*Gladness fills the world today;*
*From the tomb that could not hold Him,*
*See, the stone is rolled away!*

## *Did You Know?*

Scholars cannot be certain where the name "Easter" came from, but there are several theories that seem probable to Christians. Some believe it comes from the word *east,* since the sun rises from that direction. Others suggest it comes from the word *oster,* which means to rise. Whatever its origins, Easter is a time to celebrate the new life that Jesus bought for us with His suffering, death, and victorious resurrection!

## Celebrate the Gift of New Life!

I asked God for all things
so I could enjoy life.
He gave me life so
I could enjoy all things.

*Death hath no more
dominion over him.*

ROMANS 6:9 KJV

*Easter says you can
put truth in a grave,
but it won't stay there.*

## Did You Know?

For three centuries after the Resurrection of Christ, different groups celebrated Easter on different dates. However, in A.D. 325, a group of Christians gathered in Niceaea to determine an official date for the holiday. The Council of Niceaea decided that Easter would always fall on the Sunday following the first full moon on or after the vernal (spring) equinox.

*Did You Know?*

The equinox is a day when the hours of sunlight and darkness are equal. It comes twice a year—fall and spring. The vernal equinox usually falls on March 20. Therefore, Easter may fall on any Sunday between March 22 and April 25. About one fourth of the time it falls in March; the rest of the time it falls in April.

*Jesus said, . . . "I am the resurrection
and the life.
He who believes in me will live,
even though he dies;
and whoever lives and believes
in me will never die."*

JOHN 11:25–26

The God of our fathers
raised Jesus from the dead—
whom you had killed by
hanging him on a tree.
God exalted him to his own right hand as
Prince and Savior that he might give
repentance and forgiveness of sins.

ACTS 5:30–31

Easter says to us that despite
everything to the contrary,
His will for us will prevail,
love will prevail over hate,
justice over injustice and oppression,
peace over exploitation and bitterness.

*The best news
the world ever had
came from a graveyard.*

# *Lent*

The season leading up to Easter is called *Lent*. It begins on Ash Wednesday—forty-six days before Easter Sunday. For many Christians, the Lenten season is a time for fasting and repentance. This is in anticipation of the celebration of the glorious gift of forgiveness that came with Jesus' resurrection on Easter. Fasting is suspended on Sundays, leaving forty days. This is intended to remind Christians of the forty days Jesus fasted in the wilderness.

Repentance is an ongoing process.
One must be forever repentant.
It is not enough to once feel sorrow over sin.
True repentance affects the whole man
and alters the entire lifestyle.

# The Proper Lenten Fast

"Is this the kind of fast I have chosen,

only a day for a man to humble himself?

Is it only for bowing one's head like a reed

and for lying on sackcloth and ashes?

Is that what you call a fast, a day acceptable to the Lord?

Is not this the kind of fasting I have chosen:

to loose the chains of injustice and untie the cords of the yoke,

to set the oppressed free and break every yoke?

Is it not to share your food with the hungry

and to provide the poor wanderer with shelter—

when you see the naked, to clothe him,
and not to turn away from your own flesh and blood?
Then your light will break forth like the dawn,
and your healing will quickly appear;
then your righteousness will go before you,
and the glory of the Lord will be your rear guard.
Then you will call, and the Lord will answer;
you will cry for help, and he will say: Here am I."

ISAIAH 58:5-9

# *Lenten Prayer*

Jesus, Blessed Savior, be with me this Lent and always.
Sustain and strengthen me to carry the crosses life sends my way,
all so small compared to the cross You bore.
Open my eyes to the burdens others bear and show me how to
reach out to them with Your own love and care.
Remind me that all my crosses are small
when You carry them with me.
Lead me, guide me, this Lent and always.
Amen.

*I remember two things:*
*that I am a great sinner*
*and that Christ is a great Savior.*

# Ash Wednesday

Ash Wednesday is the beginning of the Lenten season when Christians confess their sins, cleanse their hearts, and confirm the presence of Christ in their lives. Its official name is Day of Ashes. It is customary during an Ash Wednesday service in some churches for the minister to dip a finger in the dish filled with ashes and draw small crosses on the foreheads of penitents. The Lenten season is actually a time of deep thankfulness for the riches of God's forgiveness, which the Cross symbolizes.

*Did You Know?*

Ashes have been a sign of mourning and repentance since earliest biblical times. Individuals wore sackcloth, a course fabric made of flax or hemp, sat on the ground, and covered their heads with ashes to demonstrate their sorrow.

# Celebrate God's Love for You!

Easter is a day to fan the ashes of dead hope, a day to banish doubts and seek the slopes where the sun is rising, to revel in the faith that transports us out of ourselves and the dead past into the vast and inviting future. For we have a future with a God who loves us enough to give His very life for us. When we celebrate Easter, we celebrate God's love.

# Ash Wednesday Tradition

In many countries, it is customary to make and eat tiny pretzels on Ash Wednesday. The word pretzel is derived from a Latin word that means "little arms," and the shape of the pretzel is thought to represent arms folded in prayer. Part of what we celebrate at Easter is the privilege of free access into God's presence, which Jesus earned for us with His death and resurrection.

# Mothering Sunday

The fourth Sunday in Lent is called Mid-Lent Sunday or Mothering Sunday in England. On this day, children visit their mothers and present them with gifts and flowers. The origin of this holiday is not known with certainty, but many believe it is rooted in the honor Jesus showed His mother while He was on the cross.

*Near the cross of Jesus stood his mother . . .
When Jesus saw his mother there and the
disciple whom he loved standing nearby,
he said to his mother, "Dear woman,
here is your son," and to the disciple,
"Here is your mother." From that time on,
this disciple took her into his home.*

JOHN 19:25–27

*Did You Know?*

Mothering Sunday was the forerunner of Mother's Day. Presenting mothers with gifts and wearing carnations—white in memory of mothers who had passed on and red in honor of those still living—were ideas taken from the original mother's holiday.

*"Honor your father and mother"— which is the first commandment with a promise— "that it may go well with you and that you may enjoy long life on the earth."*

EPHESIANS 6:2–3

*Did You Know?*

In the first century after Christ's Resurrection, Christians called the week before Easter "White Week." Many new believers were baptized during this time, and Christians wore white clothing as a sign of their new lives.

## *Did You Know?*

White Week, which coincides with the final week of Lent, is also called Holy Week or Passion Week. The word "passion" in this context means suffering. It is a time for Christians to remember the final days of Jesus' earthly life and ministry. The week begins with Palm Sunday and includes Maundy Thursday and Good Friday.

This week is also a time of celebration as we remember Jesus' determination to rescue us from captivity to sin, making it possible for us to joyfully anticipate spending eternity with Him in heaven.

# Palm Sunday

Palm Sunday marks the day that Jesus came into Jerusalem for the last time. As He rode on the back of a donkey, the crowds threw palm branches across His path. This was a common practice intended to honor important visitors to the city. For the Jews, palm branches were a symbol of elegance and grace.

*The great crowd that had come for the Feast heard that Jesus was on his way to Jerusalem. They took palm branches and went out to meet him, shouting, "Hosanna! Blessed is he who comes in the name of the Lord!"*

JOHN 12:12–13

*Did You Know?*

In some countries, small pieces of dried palm are twisted and tied to form crosses. These are often distributed to the people during the Palm Sunday church service. Others make them for themselves and pin them to their clothing.

*Ride on! Ride on in majesty!*
*In lowly pomp ride on to die:*
*Bow thy meek head to mortal pain:*
*Then take, O God, thy power and reign.*

# Holiday Traditions

The Gleason family of Michigan use green construction paper to make palm branches, which they give to their friends on Palm Sunday.

Instructions: Fold the paper in half, lengthwise. Begin at the fold on the top and cut an arc that ends at the center of the paper about a quarter inch from the fold. From there, cut downward parallel to the fold. On the top half, cut narrow lines inward almost to the fold. Open up and you have a palm branch to share.

*Did You Know?*

When palm branches are not available, a number of substitutes can be used. These include boxwood, willow, pussy willow, olive, myrtle, bay, and even the herb Rosemary.

*Hosanna, loud hosanna,*
*The little children sang;*
*Through pillared court and temple*
*The lovely anthem rang;*
*To Jesus, who had blessed them*
*Close folded to His breast,*
*The children sang their praises,*
*The simplest and the best.*

From Olivet they followed
'Mid an exultant crowd,
The victor palm branch waving,
And chanting clear and loud;
The Lord of men and angels
Rode on in lowly state,
Nor scorned that little children
Should on His bidding wait.

# Maundy Thursday

Maundy Thursday celebrates the night when Jesus shared His last meal with His disciples. The word *maundy,* a Latin word, means command. It refers to one of the last commands Jesus gave His disciples on that night—to love each other. He was getting ready to show them just how great His love for them was.

*"My command is this: Love each other as I have loved you. Greater love has no one than this, that he lay down his life for his friends. You are my friends if you do what I command."*

JOHN 15:12–14

# Holiday Traditions

On the Thursday prior to His crucifixion, before Jesus ate
His last meal with His disciples, He insisted on washing
their feet. Foot washing is an important element of the
Maundy Thursday celebration. On that night in many
churches, pastors wash the feet of the members of their
congregation to follow Christ's example of humble service.

*[Jesus] got up from the meal, took off his outer clothing, and wrapped a towel around his waist. After that, he poured water into a basin and began to wash his disciples' feet, drying them with the towel that was wrapped around him.*

JOHN 13:4–5

# *Holiday Traditions*

It is customary for Christians to share Communion on
Maundy Thursday, repeating the words that Jesus spoke to
His disciples as they shared the Passover meal on the night
before He died. Many find this service inspiring as they
realize how much God was willing to endure just for them.

*[Jesus] took bread, gave thanks and broke it,
and gave it to them, saying, "This is my
body given for you; do this in remembrance
of me." In the same way, after the supper
he took the cup, saying, "This cup
is the new covenant in my blood,
which is poured out for you."*

LUKE 22:19-20

47

*[Jesus] then began to teach them that the Son of Man must suffer many things and be rejected by the elders, chief priests and teachers of the law, and that he must be killed and after three days rise again.*

MARK 8:31

Hallelujah! Hallelujah!
On the third morning He arose,
Bright with victory o'er his foes.
Sing we lauding,
And applauding,
Hallelujah!

## *Did You Know?*

Church bells ring on Maundy Thursday and then remain silent during the days commemorating Christ's "passion" or suffering. They are rung again on Easter Sunday morning to signal the glorious Resurrection that gave hope to a captive world.

*It was love that kept Jesus from calling 12,000 angels who had already drawn their swords to come to His rescue.*

# Good Friday

Good Friday is the most solemn day of the year for Christians. Christ's death and suffering is remembered on this day. It commemorates the events of that day long ago, when Jesus was betrayed, arrested, tried, beaten, and put to death on a cross. This astounding event—when God gave himself up for sacrifice for the sins of the world—demonstrates that God is so in love with His people that He will go to great lengths to insure their happiness.

# The Key to Life!

The cross is a picture of violence,
yet the key to peace,
a picture of suffering,
yet the key to healing,
a picture of death,
yet the key to life.

*He wore a crown of thorns that you might wear
a crown of glory; and was nailed to the cross
with His arms wide open, to show with what
freeness all His merits will be bestowed on you and
how heartily He will receive you into His heart.*

[LANGUAGE UPDATED]

*The soldiers twisted together a crown
of thorns and put it on his head.
They clothed him in a purple robe and
went up to him again and again, saying,
"Hail, king of the Jews!"*

JOHN 19:2–3

When He gave Himself,
He gave me back my self
that I had lost.

*Finally Pilate handed him over to them to be crucified. The soldiers took charge of Jesus. Carrying his own cross, he went out to the place of the Skull (which in Aramaic is called Golgotha). Here they crucified him, and with him two others— one on each side and Jesus in the middle.*

JOHN 19:16–18

'Twas a thief that said
the last kind word to Christ:
Christ took the kindness
and forgave the theft.

One of the criminals who hung there hurled insults at him: "Aren't
you the Christ? Save yourself and us!"
But the other criminal rebuked him. "Don't you fear God,"
he said, "since you are under the same sentence?
We are punished justly, for we are getting what our deeds deserve.
But this man has done nothing wrong."
Then he said, "Jesus, remember me when
you come into your kingdom."
Jesus answered him, "I tell you the truth,
today you will be with me in paradise."

LUKE 23:39-43

Joy is distinctly a Christian word and a Christian thing. It is the reverse of happiness. Happiness is the result of what happens of an agreeable sort. Joy has its springs deep down inside. And that spring never runs dry, no matter what happens. Only Jesus gives that joy. He had joy, singing its music within, even under the shadow of the cross.

There was no other good enough
To pay the price of sin,
He only could unlock the gate,
Of heaven and let us in.
O dearly, dearly, He has loved,
We must love Him too,
Trust in His redeeming blood,
And try His works to do.

## *Did You Know?*

It was customary in Old England for blacksmiths to refuse to hammer nails into horseshoes on Good Friday. Household chores that used nails were also suspended. This custom was intended to show respect for Jesus, whose hands were nailed to the cross.

*[Jesus] was handed over to you by God's set purpose and foreknowledge; and you, with the help of wicked men, put him to death by nailing him to the cross. But God raised him from the dead, freeing him from the agony of death, because it was impossible for death to keep its hold on him.*

ACTS 2:23–24

# Holiday Traditions

Planting seeds has long been a beloved Good Friday tradition. Seeds of any kind can be planted in the garden, a window box, or even a pot. While children cover the seeds with soil, they should be told that the seeds represent the body of the Lord Jesus Christ being buried. Then they are reminded that in a matter of days the seeds will burst through the soil, just as Christ burst from His burial tomb in victory over sin and death that saved us all.

Jesus replied, "The hour has come for the Son of Man to be glorified. I tell you the truth, unless a kernel of wheat falls to the ground and dies, it remains only a single seed. But if it dies, it produces many seeds."

JOHN 12:23–24

*Rejoice in the Lord always.*
*I will say it again: Rejoice!*

PHILIPPIANS 4:4

*[Jesus said], "Now is your time of grief,*
*but I will see you again and you will rejoice,*
*and no one will take away your joy.*

JOHN 16:22

*God forbid that I should glory,*
*save in the cross of our*
*Lord Jesus Christ.*

GALATIANS 6:14 KJV

This is the secret of joy.
We shall no longer strive for our
own way, but commit ourselves,
easily and simply, to God's way,
acquiesce in His will, and
in so doing, find our peace.

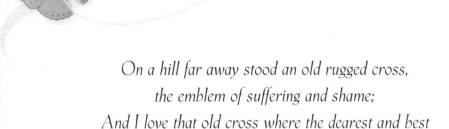

*On a hill far away stood an old rugged cross,*
*the emblem of suffering and shame;*
*And I love that old cross where the dearest and best*
*For a world of lost sinners was slain.*

*[Jesus] said, "I, when I am
lifted up from the earth,
will draw all men to myself."*

JOHN 12:32

God proved His love on the cross.
When Christ hung and bled,
and died, it was God saying
to the world—I love you!

# Holiday Traditions

Hot Cross Buns are traditionally served for breakfast on Good Friday. The tops are marked with a white icing cross to remind us of Christ's victory over death.

# Hot Cross Buns

1 cup milk, scalded
½ cup sugar
3 tbsp melted butter
½ tsp salt
1 pkg dry yeast
½ cup warm water
1 egg, well beaten
3 cups flour
1 tsp cinnamon
½ cup raisins
1 tsp grated orange peel
1 cup powdered sugar
2 tsp milk

Mix together milk, sugar, butter, and salt. Let cool. Dissolve yeast in warm water. Add yeast and egg to mixture. Stir in flour and cinnamon. Add raisins and orange peel. Let rise for 1 hour. Shape dough into round balls and place on a cookie sheet. With a sharp knife, cut a cross on the top of each one. Bake at 400 degrees for 20 minutes. After cooling, drizzle with powdered sugar and milk mixture.

*Did You Know?*

Though generally performed at Christmastime, George Frideric Handel's *Messiah* was written to tell the story of Christ's life and passion. It was first performed in England during the Lenten Season on March 23, 1743.

*Lift your voices in
triumph on high,
For Jesus is risen
and man cannot die.*

# Easter Eve

Many churches hold a special service on the night before Easter Sunday. On the stroke of midnight, a flame is passed from one person to another until each worshipper has a small, lit candle. These candles represent the life of Jesus Christ, which could not be extinguished. Rising from the grave, His flame was rekindled and continues to burn brightly. Light conquered darkness; life conquered death.

Thou art the Sun
of other days,
They shine by giving
back thy rays.

If Easter means anything to modern man, it means that truth is eternal. You may nail it to the tree, wrap it up in grave clothes, and seal it in a tomb; but "truth crushed to earth, shall rise again."

The edges of God are tragedy;
the depths of God are
joy, beauty, resurrection, life.

**Resurrection answers crucifixion;**
**life answers death.**

*While Jesus was on the cross, God sat on his hands.*
*He turned His back. He ignored*
*the screams of the innocent.*
*He sat in silence while the sins of the*
*world were placed upon His son . . . .*
*Was it right? No.*
*Was it fair? No.*
*Was it love? Yes.*

What language shall I borrow
To thank Thee dearest Friend,
For this Thy dying sorrow,
    Thy pity without end?
Oh, make me Thine forever;
    And should I fainting be,
Lord, let me never, never
Outlive my love to Thee!

In vain with stone the cave they barred;
In vain the watch kept ward and guard;
Majestic from the spoiled tomb.
In pomp of triumph Christ is come.

The stone at the tomb of Jesus
was a pebble to the
Rock of Ages inside.

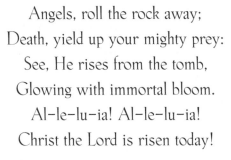

Angels, roll the rock away;
Death, yield up your mighty prey:
See, He rises from the tomb,
Glowing with immortal bloom.
Al-le-lu-ia! Al-le-lu-ia!
Christ the Lord is risen today!

*He will swallow up death in victory;*
*and the Lord GOD will wipe*
*away tears from off all faces.*

ISAIAH 25:8 KJV

All Christian worship is a witness
of the resurrection of Him who liveth
for ever and ever. Because He lives,
"now abideth faith, hope, charity."

*If we have been united with him like this
in his death, we will certainly also be
united with him in his resurrection.*

ROMANS 6:5

# Easter Sunday

The most joyous of all Christian holidays, Easter Sunday celebrates Christ's victory over death and the grave. It sets Christianity apart from all other religions, for we serve a Risen Savior. So go ahead and CELEBRATE!

*Christ has turned
all our sunsets
into dawns.*

On the first day of the week, very early in the morning, the women took the spices they had prepared and went to the tomb. They found the stone rolled away from the tomb, but when they entered, they did not find the body of the Lord Jesus.

While they were wondering about this, suddenly two men in clothes that gleamed like lightning stood beside them. In their fright, the women bowed down with their faces to the ground, but the men said to them. "Why do you look for the living among the dead? He is not here; he has risen!

LUKE 24:1-6

Lo! Jesus meets us, risen from the tomb;
Lovingly He greets us, scatters fear and gloom;
Let the Church with gladness hymns of triumph sing.
For her Lord now lives, death has lost its sting.
Yours be the glory,
Risen, conquering Son,
Endless is the victory
You o'er death have won.

*"This Jesus God raised up,
and of that all of us
are witnesses."*

ACTS 2:32 NRSV

95

Christianity stands or falls
with the resurrection, and this
single factor makes Christianity
remarkably one of a kind.

*There are only two essential requirements:*
*First: Has any one cheated death and proved it?*
*Second: Is it available to me?*
*Here is the complete record.*
*Confucius' tomb—occupied*
*Buddha's tomb—occupied*
*Mohammed's tomb—occupied*
*Jesus' tomb—empty!*

# Holiday Traditions

The Morgan family of Oklahoma remembers getting a new pair of shoes each year during Easter week. The children put on their shoes for the first time while dressing for the Easter Sunday service. As they put on the shoes, their mother had them repeat the phrase, "Today I walk in newness of life!"

The great Easter truth is not that
we are to live newly after death,
but that we are to be new here and
now by the power of the resurrection.

The Lord is risen indeed!
And are the tidings true?
Yes, we beheld the Savior bleed,
And saw Him living, too.

The Lord is risen indeed!
Then hell has lost his prey;
With Him is risen the ransomed seed
To reign in endless day.

The Lord is risen indeed!
He lives, to die no more;
He lives, the sinner's cause to plead,
Whose curse and shame He bore.

Then take your golden lyres,
And strike each cheerful chord;
Join, all ye bright celestial choirs,
To sing our risen Lord.

# Holiday Traditions

The chiming of bells has called people to worship for centuries. But this custom is especially significant on Easter Sunday. The ringing of bells remind penitents that the time of fasting and repentance is over and the joyful celebration of Christ's victory over death has begun. In some countries, the bells continue to peel from morning until night with only short pauses for celebration and reflection.

*O chime of sweet Saint Charity,*
*Peal soon that Easter morn*
*When Christ for all shall risen be,*
*And in all hearts new-born!*

# Holiday Traditions

An "Easter branch" is a simple branch or twig that has begun to sprout new buds or leaves. It can be taken from any tree except evergreens. The emphasis should be on displaying the nice, new growth. Choose long branches that can be laid along the mantle, table, or buffet.

They can also be displayed in a tall vase with spring flowers such as lilies and daffodils to celebrate new life that comes to us because of Jesus' victory over death.

Our Lord has written the
promise of resurrection,
not in books alone, but
in every leaf in springtime.

# Holiday Traditions

Eggs are the traditional decoration for Easter. The contents can be removed by punching a small hole in each end of the egg. Blow slowly but firmly into one end, and the contents will come out the other. Dip the egg shells in bright colors of Easter egg dye and then add Christian symbols, such as crosses, Alpha and Omega symbols, flowers, or inscriptions like "Christ is Risen." These symbols can remind us that Jesus is the reason we celebrate, and our rescue from the penalty and power of sin is reason to celebrate indeed!

# *Holiday Traditions*

The Lansing family of Florida puts Scripture verses inside
plastic eggs and mixes them in with eggs filled with candy and
small coins. When the children come in from their Easter egg
hunt, they open the eggs and read the Scriptures aloud.

# Easter Biscuits

Easter biscuits are a great idea for breakfast on Easter morning. The day before, mix up the dough and roll it out on a floured board. Cut the dough in the shape of eggs, bunnies, and chicks, and decorate them as you would cookies. If you prefer a more sacred symbol, cut the dough in the shape of small crosses. Serve them on Easter morning as one more celebratory reminder of the great gift of God, our salvation.

8 oz Self-rising flour
4 oz Margarine
4 oz Granulated sugar
pinch of salt
1 tsp Cinnamon
1 egg

Cut the margarine into the flour. Add sugar, salt, and cinnamon and mix.
Add egg and work the dough with your hands until it becomes pliable. Bake
at 350 degrees until golden brown.

*Oh, my Savior make me see*
*how dearly Thou*
*has paid for me.*

Our old history ends
with the cross;
our new history begins
with the resurrection.

*Low in the grave he lay*
*Jesus, my Savior!*
*Waiting the coming day*
*Jesus, my Lord!*
*Up from the grave He arose,*
*With a mighty triumph o'er His foes.*
*He arose a Victor from the dark domain,*
*And He lives forever with His saints to reign.*
*He arose! He arose!*
*Hallelujah! Christ arose!*

*Death cannot keep his prey*
*Jesus, my Savior!*
*He tore the bars away*
*Jesus, my Lord!*
*Up from the grave He arose,*
*With a mighty triumph o'er His foes.*
*He arose a Victor from the dark domain,*
*And He lives forever with His saints to reign.*
*He arose! He arose!*
*Hallelujah! Christ arose!*

# Easter Monday

Many parts of the world celebrate the day after Easter Sunday. Some call it Great Monday, others call it Dyngus Day. Dyngus comes from the Latin word *dignus,* which means worthy or honored. Many new believers choose to be baptized on this day.

We believe that as in baptism
we have been united with Christ
in His death and resurrection,
so we have died to sin and
should walk in newness of life.

*All of us who were baptized into Christ Jesus were baptized into his death? We were therefore buried with him through baptism into death in order that, just as Christ was raised from the dead through the glory of the Father, we too may live a new life.*

ROMANS 6:3-4

*Come, ye saints, look here and wonder,*
*See the place where Jesus lay;*
*He has burst His bands asunder;*
*He has borne our sins away;*
*Joyful tidings,*
*Yes, the Lord has risen to-day.*

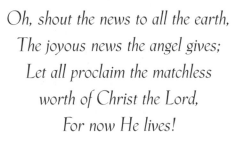

*Oh, shout the news to all the earth,*
*The joyous news the angel gives;*
*Let all proclaim the matchless*
*worth of Christ the Lord,*
*For now He lives!*

*Oh, sing the glad, triumphant strain,*
*The song of victory o'er the grave;*
*Let all rejoice with loud refrain*
*That Jesus lives with power to save.*

No person hearing the story of the resurrection can possibly be any more skeptical of it than were the apostles when they first heard about it. The record shows that Jesus had to go to great lengths to overcome their disbelief. Once he ate an impromptu meal of cold fish and honeycomb—the only food at hand—to demonstrate to one diehard doubter that he wasn't a ghost.

"Christ the Lord is risen today,"
Sons of men and angels say.
Raise your joys and triumphs high;
Sing, ye heavens, and earth reply.

*In the bonds of Death He lay*
*Who for our offence was slain;*
*But the Lord is risen to-day,*
*Christ hath brought us life again,*
*Wherefore let us all rejoice.*
*Singing loud, with cheerful voice,*
*Hallelujah!*

*Tomb, thou shalt not hold Him longer;*
*Death is strong, but Life is stronger;*
*Stronger than the dark, the light;*
*Stronger than the wrong, the right;*
*Faith and Hope triumphant say*
*Christ will rise on Easter Day.*

# Holiday Traditions

The English have an old custom called "lifting" or "heaving," which was a favorite on Easter Monday. Intended to celebrate Jesus rising from the dead, the young men would decorate a chair with flowers and greenery and carry it around the village to the homes of their friends and family. The women in each house were lifted in the chair three times—the number of days Jesus was in the tomb. On Tuesday, the women took the chair around and lifted the men.

*[Jesus said], "For as Jonah was three days
and three nights in the belly of a huge fish,
so the Son of Man will be three days and
three nights in the heart of the earth."*

MATTHEW 12:40

# Easter Pretzels

1 ½ cups warm water

1 package yeast

1 tsp salt

1 Tbsp sugar

4 cups flour

1 egg

In a large mixing bowl, sprinkle yeast on the water and stir until dissolved. Add salt, sugar, and flour to mixture and stir until it forms a soft dough. Knead the dough. Break it into small balls and roll with your hands until they form a thin rope. Twist in the shape of a pretzel and place on a cookie sheet. Brush with beaten egg. Cook at 425 degrees for 15 minutes.

# Easter Flowers

Known as the "white-robed apostles of hope," Easter lilies are the most celebrated of all the holiday flowers. The beautiful white lilies were found growing in the Garden of Gethsemane, where Jesus prayed on the night before His crucifixion. Legend has it that they sprang up where drops of sweat fell from Jesus' brow as he agonized over what lay ahead of Him. The lily blossom appears to be down-turned in sorrow. But best of all is the beautiful perfume, an aroma that is acceptable to God as a reminder of Jesus' sacrifice for us.

*Being in anguish, [Jesus] prayed
more earnestly, and his sweat was like
drops of blood falling to the ground.*

LUKE 22:44

# Easter Flowers

Legend has it that wood from the Dogwood tree was used to make the cross on which Christ was crucified. The truth of this is not known. But the tree does display four beautiful white petals on each blossom. Each petal bears a dark red stain along the outer edge, and at the center of each bloom is what appears to be a tiny crown of thorns. Nature celebrates God's great gift every spring with such shows.

*After they had mocked him, they took
off the robe and put his own clothes on him.
Then they led him away to crucify him.*

MATTHEW 27:31

*Awake, thou wintry earth—*
*Fling off thy sadness!*
*Fair vernal flowers, laugh forth*
*Your ancient gladness!*

*O Risen Christ! O Easter Flower!*
*How dear Thy Grace has grown!*
*From east to west, with loving power.*
*Make all the world Thine own.*

Spring bursts today,
for Christ is risen and
all the earth's at play.

# *Holiday Traditions*

The Stafford family of Iowa loves to make Easter cookies with their children. These cookies demonstrate the death, burial, and resurrection of Jesus Christ. Ingredients needed: 1 tsp vinegar, 3 egg whites, pinch of salt, 1 cup sugar. Preheat oven to 300 degrees. (See the next page.)

# *Easter Cookie Demonstration*

- Put the vinegar in a bowl and let the children smell it. Tell the children that Jesus was thirsty on the cross so the soldiers gave him vinegar to drink. Read John 19:28–30.

- Add egg whites. Tell the children that these represent life—Jesus gave His life that we could live. Read John 10:10–23.

- Let the children taste the salt. Tell them that it represents tears shed by those people who loved Jesus. Read Luke 23:27.

- Add sugar. Tell the children that the sugar represents the sweetest part of the story. Jesus died because He loves us and wants us to know Him. Read 1 John 4:8 and John 3:16

(Continued on next page)

- Beat on high for 2–5 minutes. Tell the children that the batter is white to show us how our hearts will look after we are forgiven of our sins. Read Isaiah 1:18.

- Place spoonfuls of batter on a cookie sheet. Place in oven and turn oven OFF. Tape the door shut. Tell the children that this represents how Jesus' body was sealed in the tomb. Read Matthew 27:57–60.

- Open the oven on Easter morning, pass out the cookies to the children. As they bite into the cookies, they will find that they are hollow on the inside. Tell them that this represents that the tomb was empty and Jesus is alive. Read Matthew 28:1–9.

# Ascension Sunday—
## The Celebration Continues!

Ascension Day—a Thursday, the fortieth day after Easter Sunday—celebrates the return of the Lord Jesus to heaven. After showing himself to His followers on a number of occasions, Jesus called them to a mountaintop, spoke to them briefly, and, as they watched, ascended into heaven. Ascension Sunday is the Sunday following Ascension Day.

*When [Jesus] had led them out to the vicinity of Bethany, he lifted up his hands and blessed them. While he was blessing them, he left them and was taken up into heaven. Then they worshipped him and returned to Jerusalem with great joy.*

LUKE 24:50–52

# Holiday Traditions

The Liota family of Tennessee celebrates Ascension Sunday by gathering with friends and family members on a hill near their home. They go early in the morning, sing hymns, and read the passage describing Christ's ascension into heaven.

The air is like a butterfly
With frail blue wings.
The happy earth looks at the sky
And sings.

# Pentecost Sunday

Pentecost simply means "fiftieth" in Greek. It is the Sunday seven weeks or fifty days after Easter Sunday. It commemorates the coming of the Holy Spirit, which Jesus promised to His followers before His ascension into heaven. This is a wonderful time to celebrate the gift that Jesus bought for us with His life: that God himself would dwell within us!

When the day of Pentecost was fully come,
they were all with one accord in one place.
And suddenly there came a sound from
heaven as of a rushing mighty wind,
and it filled all the house where
they were sitting. And there appeared
unto them cloven tongues like as of fire,
and it sat upon each of them.

ACTS 2:1–3 KJV

143

The Comforter has come!
The Comforter has come!
The Holy Ghost from heaven,
The Father's promise given!
Oh, spread the tidings 'round,
Wherever man is found:
The Comforter has come!

*Did You Know?*

The *wind* is the primary symbol for the Holy Spirit. This is because the biblical account of the Holy Spirit filling the believers on the Day of Pentecost describes it as the sound of a "rushing, mighty wind."

# Holiday Traditions

The Ernesto family of Texas celebrates Pentecost Sunday by taking their kites to a nearby park. Each kite has the name of a family member written across it. Before they put their kites in the air, the children are told that the Holy Spirit moves in their lives just as the wind moves their kites—powerfully and yet unseen!

# Holiday Traditions

The Robinson family of Michigan celebrates Pentecost Sunday by hanging wind chimes outside doors and windows. All year long, family members search for an appropriate wind chime to add to their collection. Early on Pentecost Sunday, the entire family gathers to hang the chimes. The children are told that the beautiful sounds made by the wind blowing through the chimes represent the beautiful work of the Holy Spirit in their lives.

Come, Holy Spirit
Fill the hearts of your faithful
Come among us as wind and fire
And ignite our lives with renewed faith.

Come, Holy Spirit
Fill the hearts of your faithful
Be the wind and fire that brings
new life to your church
And open our minds and hearts
to your presence among us.

*Jesus himself stood among them and said to them, "Peace be with you." They were startled and frightened, thinking they saw a ghost. He said to them, "Why are you troubled, and why do doubts rise in your minds? Look at my hands and my feet. It is I myself! Touch me and see; a ghost does not have flesh and bones, as you see I have."*

When he had said this, he showed them his hands and feet. And while they still did not believe it because of joy and amazement, he asked them, "Do you have anything here to eat?" They gave him a piece of broiled fish, and he took it and ate it in their presence.

[Jesus] said to them, "This is what I told you while I was still with you: Everything must be fulfilled that is written about me in the Law of Moses, the Prophets and the Psalms." Then he opened their minds so they could understand the Scriptures.

[Jesus] told them, "This is what is written:
The Christ will suffer and rise from the dead
on the third day, and repentance and
forgiveness of sins will be preached in his
name to all nations, beginning at Jerusalem.
You are witnesses of these things. I am
going to send you what my Father has
promised; but stay in the city until you have
been clothed with power from on high."

LUKE 24:36-49

# *Easter Prayer*

Glory and praise to You, Risen Savior, for You bring light to our darkness,
joy to our sorrow, and the fullness of love to our reluctant hearts.
Once and for all You have conquered sin and evil.
In the glory of Your Resurrection we have been
set free from all that keeps us from following You.
On this Easter Day, fill our hearts with Your Light and Grace
that we might joyfully echo the words of Your Holy Angels:

He is not here in the tomb:
He is risen!
Alleluia! Alleluia!
Amen.

*O death, where is thy sting?*
*O grave, where is thy victory?*

1 CORINTHIANS 15:55 KJV

*May the glad dawn, of Easter morn*
*bring joy to thee.*
*May the calm eve of Easter leave*
*a peace divine with thee.*
*May Easter night,*
*On thine heart write,*
*O Christ, I live for Thee.*

*If you confess with your mouth,*
*"Jesus is Lord," and*
*believe in your heart that*
*God raised him from the dead,*
*you will be saved.*

ROMANS 10:9

# Acknowledgments

(6) John Greenleaf Whittier, (7) Fanny Crosby, (11) Clarence W. Hull, (16) Desmond Tutu, (17,156) Author Unknown, (19) Richard Owen Roberts, (22,148–49,154) St. Michael's Parish, (23) John Newton, (37) Henry Hart Milman, (40–41) Jennette Threlfall, (49) 12th Century Latin, (51,72) Billy Graham, (53) David Watson, (54) John Bunyan, (56) Bernard of Clairvaux, (58) Robert Browning, (60) Samuel Dickey Gordon, (61) Cecil Frances Alexander, (69) Evelyn Underhill, (70) George Bennard, (77) Henry Ware, (79) John Keble, (80) Donald Harvey Tippet, (81) Marjorie Hewitt Suchocki, (82) Max Lucado, (85) Frederick Beck, (86) Thomas Scott, (88) Lyman Abbott, (91) Clement of Alexandria, (94) Edmund Louis Budry, (96) Steve Kumar, (97) G.B. Hardy, (99,123,133) Phillips Brooks, (100–01, 117) Thomas Kelly, (103) James Russell Lowell, (105,122) Martin Luther, (110) Richard Crashaw, (111) Watchman Nee, (112–13) Robert Lowry, (115) Moravian Covenant for Christian Living, (118–19) Hugh C. Benner, (120) Louis Cassels, (121) Charles Wesley, (132) Thomas Blackburn, (134) Christina Georgina Rossetti, (141) Joyce Kilmer, (144) Wm. J. Kirkpatrick

If you have enjoyed this book or it has impacted your life,
we would like to hear from you.

Please contact us at:

Honor Books
4050 Lee Vance View
Colorado Springs, CO 80918

Or by e-mail at www.cookministries.com